THE TOP SECRET HISTORY OF
CODES AND
CODE BREAKING

ROY APPS

WAYLAND
www.waylandbooks.co.uk

With thanks to the students of Oakley School.

First published in Great Britain in 2016 by Wayland
Text copyright © Wayland 2016
All rights reserved.
A CIP catalogue record for this book is available from the British Library.

Editor: Hayley Fairhead
Designer: Kevin Knight

Photo acknowledgements: p1(rpt) wikimedia.org, p3(rpt) Bernhard Classen/Alamy Stock Photo, p4(b) Ancient Art & Architecture Collection Ltd/Alamy Stock Photo, p4 Shutterstock.com, p5 Kevin Knight, p6(t) PRISMA ARCHIVO/Alamy Stock Photo, p6(b) and p30(t) Shutterstock.com, p2 and p7(t) Kevin Knight, p7(b) Shutterstock.com, p8 DeAgostini/Getty Images, p3 and p9(t) Bernhard Classen/Alamy Stock Photo, p9(b) John Alston, p10 A. Astes/Alamy Stock Photo, p11 Shutterstock.com, p12 Classic Image/Alamy Stock Photo, p13 wikipedia, p14(tr) Art Directors & TRIP/Alamy Stock Photo, page 14(bl) and p30(bl) Shutterstock.com, p16(t) wikimedia.org, p16(b) Universal Images Group North America LLC/Alamy Stock Photo, p18(t) Kevin Knight, p18 Jan Kruger/Getty Images, p19 Kevin Knight, p20(t) Shutterstock.com, p20(b) Shutterstock.com, p20(b) Shutterstock.com, p21 Shutterstock.com, p22(t) wikimedia.org, p22(b) Pictorial Press Ltd/Alamy Stock Photo, p23 Shutterstock.com, p24(l) and p31 wikimedia.org, p24(r) Shutterstock.com, p1 and p25 wikimedia.org, p26(t) Heritage Image Partnership Ltd/Alamy Stock Photo, p26(b) Pictorial Press Ltd/Alamy Stock Photo, p27 Jon Lewis/Alamy Stock Photo, p28(t) Shutterstock.com, p28(b) Google via Getty Images, p30(rpt) wikimedia.org, detective image throughout Shutterstock.com.

ISBN: 978 0 7502 9885 8

Printed in China

MIX
Paper from
responsible sources
FSC
www.fsc.org   FSC® C104740

Wayland
An imprint of Hachette Children's Book Group
Carmelite House
50 Victoria Embankment
London EC4Y 0DZ
An Hachette UK Company
www.hachette.co.uk

Did you crack the code on the cover?

Did you find the message in the QR code (underneath the word 'APPS')?

TOP SECRET INFO
The Morse Code (top left) says:

TOP SECRET CODES SMART KIDS ONLY!
The QR code message is:

CONTENTS

Why We Need Codes (Shhh! It's a Secret)   4

Picture Codes   6

Invisible Messages   8

Gnitirw Sdrawkcab and Other Letter Codes   10

Smoke Signals and Ciphers   12

Help! My Code Has Been Cracked!   14

The Unbreakable Code   16

I Don't Understand a Word You're Saying!   18

The Most Useful Code Ever Invented   20

The Analytical Engine   22

The Enigma Machine   24

The Computer as Big as a Room   26

To Infinity and Beyond   28

Glossary   30

Further Information   31

Index   32

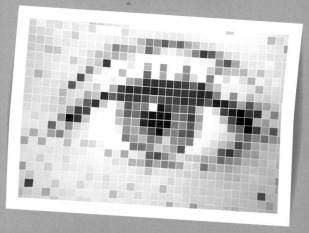

WHY WE NEED CODES
(SHHH! IT'S A SECRET!)

Since the earliest times, human beings have communicated information to each other. However, sometimes the information is so secret it has to be sent in code.

Telling Stories

Before people learned to write, they told stories to each other and passed on important information using pictures, such as cave paintings.

This painting of horses was discovered in a cave in France in 1941. It is believed to be about 17,300 years old. Maybe the artist was telling a story about his adventures out hunting. What do you think?

Secret Code

What if you need to tell someone something so special, so secret, that nobody else must know what you are saying? Maybe it's something you want a special friend to know, but no one else? Or perhaps you're an army general and you have a message for your troops about a planned attack that the enemy mustn't get hold of? Then you need a secret **code**. You must create the code and the person you are sending it to must be able to break the code to read it.

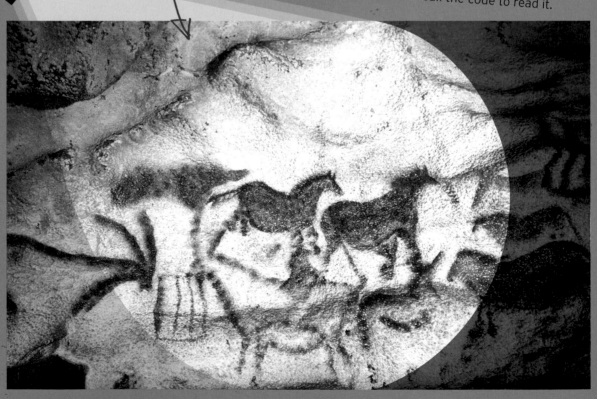

Trackers and Scouts

Lord Baden-Powell, founder of Scouting, learned
about **tracking** when he was a soldier in Africa.
Tracking is a way of leaving signs or 'picture'
messages on the ground, using sticks and stones,
that only those who know the picture code can **decipher**.
Scouts today still play tracking games.

These tracking signs mean, go this way.

Can you match these
tracking signs with
their meanings?

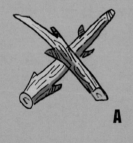

A

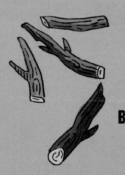

B

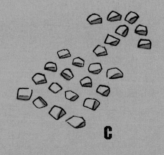

C

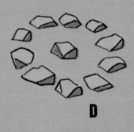

D

1 Turn left

2 Hidden message
four paces ahead

3 Not this way

4 I have gone home*

*Answers: A = 3, B = 1, C = 2, D = 4

PICTURE CODES

The Ancient Egyptians wrote in picture codes called hieroglyphs and the Maya people of Central America wrote in picture codes called glyphs.

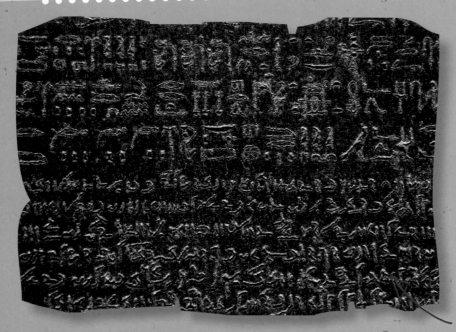

The Rosetta Stone

A huge piece of rock was dug up in 1799 by some French soldiers in Rosetta, in Egypt. They found it was covered in Ancient Egyptian writing, known as **hieroglyphs**. They had no idea what they meant. To find the true meaning of the hieroglyphs, **archaeologists** and other experts had to become code breakers.

A close-up of the hieroglyphs on the Rosetta Stone. El-Rashid is the Arabic name for the town where the Rosetta Stone was found.

Maya Glyphs

The ancient Maya wrote in **glyphs**. Maya glyphs took a long time to decipher; there are around 700 glyphs in the Maya writing code!

This glyph represents the Haab' calendar, one of a system of calendars followed by the Maya.

What is a Code?

A code is simply a way of communicating something. This: **SW1A OAA** is the postcode for the Houses of Parliament. There is nothing secret about that. It's just a way of communicating which part of London the Houses of Parliament are in.

The symbol shown on the right is a barcode, used on just about everything you buy in the supermarket. It's a way of electronically communicating the price of something at the checkout. So, not all codes are secret but they are a short and quick way of communicating information.

5 014016 150821 >

The Dancing Men

Sir Arthur Conan Doyle, who created Sherlock Holmes, was fascinated by codes and secret writing. In the story called *The Dancing Men*, Sherlock Holmes is given a letter containing this picture of 'dancing men' stick figures.

Eventually, Sherlock Holmes works out that each of the dancing men represents a different letter of the alphabet, revealing information that helps him to capture a murderer.

CODE BREAKER'S CORNER

Make Your Own Picture Code

Why not try and make your own picture code? A good way to start is to design a simple picture for each of the five vowels: A E I O U.

Here's a code using different emoticons*:

B 😄 S T 😢 F L 😜 C K

*Answer: Best of luck

7

INVISIBLE MESSAGES

Whether you're an army general trying to deceive the enemy, a criminal trying to evade the law or simply someone wanting to send a secret message to a friend, the best way to send your message is to hide it, so that it becomes invisible.

Steganography

Invisible messages have been used since ancient times. The process is called **steganography**, which comes from the Greek, meaning 'covered writing'.

A good way of using steganography is to hide your message inside another message. Can you see the hidden message in bold type shown here?*

*Answer: Call the police

Hi Charles

Lovely weat**he**r today.

Polly is coming round later.

James

The Ancient Greeks wrote secret messages on wooden or clay tablets which were then covered with wax. When the wax was melted, the secret message was revealed.

Pixels and Microdots

Other ways of writing hidden messages include using **pixels** or **microdots** (a microdot is a dot that is only about 1mm in diameter). Pixels are used to form a picture and a secret image or message can be hidden within it.

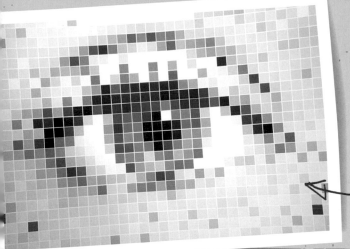

The Haircut Code

According to the Greek historian Herodotus, in the 5th century BCE a Persian ruler named Histiaeus wanted to send a secret message that he could be sure wouldn't be intercepted by his enemies. So he shaved the head of his most trusted slave and had the message tattooed on his head. As the slave made his long journey on foot, his hair grew back, but nobody guessed that there was a secret message underneath! The slave delivered his message safely.

This picture is made up of pixels. Can you see the hidden image of an eye within the picture?

Invisible Ink

Mix about ¼ cup [60ml] of bicarbonate of soda with the same amount of water. This is your invisible ink. Now dip a cotton bud or a fine brush into the mixture and write your message on a plain piece of paper. Let it dry. Finally, brush grape juice across the paper. Your secret message will appear!

GNITIRW SDRAWKCAB
AND OTHER LETTER CODES

Over the years, ancient peoples modified their writing, so that instead of lots of complicated pictures, sounds and letters became represented by simple combinations of straight and curved lines.

A statue of Julius Caesar, Emperor and code maker!

The Greek Alphabet

The first two letters in the Ancient Greek alphabet were Alpha and Beta, which is why we call this system of writing an Alphabet. Once this type of writing became common, military commanders, spies and other people who needed to send secret messages realised you didn't need haircut codes or invisible ink any more; you could simply code the letters themselves. Perhaps the simplest letter code was this: gnitirw sdrawkcab [writing backwards!].

Greek Alpha and Beta symbols

The Caesar Shift

The Roman Emperor Julius Caesar invented his own letter code. He simply moved each letter of the alphabet along four places, so that A became D and B became E and so on.

The Alphabet

A	B	C	D	E	F	G	H	I	J	K	L	M	N	O	P	Q	R	S	T	U	V	W	X	Y	Z
D	E	F	G	H	I	J	K	L	M	N	O	P	Q	R	S	T	U	V	W	X	Y	Z	A	B	C

Caesar's Code

This code became known as the Caesar Shift. Only Caesar's generals knew the code. Here's one he might have sent them. Can you decipher it? Clue: he would have sent it in 55AD and again in 43AD.

LQYDGH
EULWDLQ!*

*Answer: Invade Britain!

CODE BREAKER'S CORNER

Make Your Own Letter Code

The Caesar Shift is a **substitution cipher**. Try this substitution cipher with your friends.

Substitute the vowels in your message by moving them along one:

Vowels	Code
A E I O U	E I O U A

It's simple, just loki thos! **

Or why not make up a letter substitution code of your own!

**Answer: like this!

SMOKE SIGNALS
AND CIPHERS

The Greek army used to send messages using smoke signals. These were useful because they could be seen from great distances. However, you couldn't say a lot with a smoke signal, and it certainly wasn't secret: one puff probably meant ATTACK! and two puffs RETREAT!

Polybius' Square

A Greek army officer named Polybius hit on the idea of using pairs of soldiers holding lighted torches to send secret messages. The number of times the lighted torches were raised stood for different letters of the alphabet. He worked out his system by using a square, like the one shown here.

So to signal the word NO: Soldier 1 would give 3 flashes of his lighted torch and Soldier 2 would give three flashes of his torch to symbolise 'N'.

Then Soldier 1 would give 4 flashes of his lighted torch and Soldier 2 would give 3 flashes of his torch to symbolise 'O'.

SOLDIER 1

	1	2	3	4	5
1	A	B	C	D	E
2	F	G	H	I/J	K
3	L	M	N	O	P
4	Q	R	S	T	U
5	V	W	X	Y	Z

SOLDIER 2

You don't need two Greek solders and a couple of flaming torches to use Polybius' Square. It works just as well as a code using the numbers in the grid. Starting with the the horizontal column of letters, 'A' is written as 11, 'B' is 12, and so on to 'Z' which is written as 55. Can you break this code using Polybius' Square?

11 44 44 11 31 52 *

A form of Polybius' Square was still being used two thousand years later during the First World War.

A nineteenth century engraving showing Greeks using Polybius' Square to send messages.

Is it a Code or is it a Cipher?

A cipher is a way of sending secret messages using single letters, numbers or symbols; whereas a code is a secret message using whole words.

Here is an example of a code where certain words are used to mean something else entirely:

mustard = troops

custard = front line

You could send the following coded message:

**Put more mustard
on your custard.**

When the message is received, the decoded message will read:

**Put more troops
on your front line.**

However, 'codes' are generally accepted by code breakers to refer to any types of secret message, including ciphers and stenographs.

CODE BREAKER'S CORNER

How to Create a Pig Pen Cipher

Pig pen ciphers have been used for hundreds of years. They are called 'pig pen ciphers' because the lines in the drawing look like pens where farmers would have kept pigs! To use the code, find the letter you want to use in the grid, for example 'd'. The shape of the grid in which that letter is found then forms the shape of the code used for that letter. If the letter also has a dot underneath it, the dot is used as part of the code. This is a pig pen cipher used by the French Emperor Napoleon.

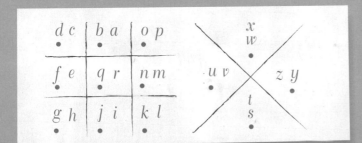

The French Emperor Napoleon used codes to communicate battle plans with his army generals.

So d is written like this: •⌐

And x is written like this: ⌄

See if you can decipher this pig pen code. Clue: you'd certainly hear it in a pig pen!*

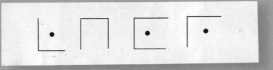

*Answer: Oink

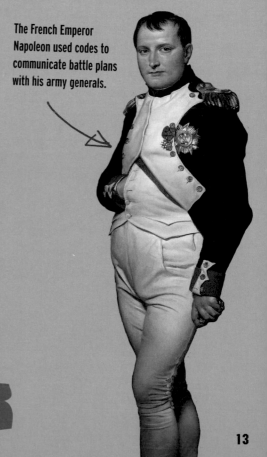

13

HELP! MY CODE HAS BEEN CRACKED!

If you know what the most common letters of the alphabet are, you can quickly begin to decode a substitution cipher.

Frequency Analysis

By looking for the most frequently used letters or symbols in a cipher, you can begin to decode it. Decoding ciphers in this way is called **frequency analysis.**

Frequency analysis was developed in the ninth century CE by the Arab mathematician Al-Kindi.

Mary Queen of Scots was executed for treason in 1587, when frequency analysis was used to stop the Babington Plot.

The Babington Plot

In 1586, Mary Queen of Scots was plotting to overthrow Queen Elizabeth I. Anthony Babington, one of Mary's supporters, sent a coded message to her, asking for permission to murder Queen Elizabeth. He used what he thought was an unbreakable substitution cipher, using symbols instead of letters. However, Sir Francis Walsingham, Queen Elizabeth's spymaster, had studied the work of Al-Kindi. He used frequency analysis to decipher the letter.

Frequency Analysis
— a Code Breaker's Guide

▶ The most common letters in the English language are: E, T, N, O, R, I, A & S

▶ The least common are Z, Q and X

▶ More than half of all English words end in E, T, D & S

▶ T is the most common first letter of a word

▶ E is the most common last letter of a word

▶ There are only two single-letter words: A and I.

CODE BREAKER'S CORNER

How to Create a Transposition Cipher

A **transposition cipher** works like this: you agree on the number of boxes in a table with your spy partner, say 6 boxes by 4 boxes. You write your message vertically in the grid boxes with no spaces between the words, starting in the left hand column:

Message: MEET ME AT THE HAUNTED CASTLE

M	M	T	A	E	S
E	E	H	U	D	T
E	A	E	N	C	L
T	T	H	T	A	E

You send the message using the letters as they appear in horizontal order:

M M T A E S E E H U D T E A E N C L T T H T A E

To decipher your message, all your spy partner needs to do is to draw an empty 6 x 4 table and fill the letters in, in a horizontal order. They will then be able to read your message vertically.

Now have a go at writing your own transposition cipher.

THE UNBREAKABLE CODE

Mathematicians and scientists who study codes and how to crack them are known as cryptologists. Knowing that frequency analysis could be used to crack substitution ciphers, cryptologists set about finding more secure ciphers.

Vigenère Cipher

In the sixteenth century, a Frenchman called Blaise de Vigenère announced to the world that he had invented an unbreakable code. He called it – what else – the Vigenère Cipher.

Blaise de Vigenère produced one of the first secure ciphers.

```
   A B C D E F G H I J K L M N O P Q R S T U V W X Y Z
A  A B C D E F G H I J K L M N O P Q R S T U V W X Y Z
B  B C D E F G H I J K L M N O P Q R S T U V W X Y Z A
C  C D E F G H I J K L M N O P Q R S T U V W X Y Z A B
D  D E F G H I J K L M N O P Q R S T U V W X Y Z A B C
E  E F G H I J K L M N O P Q R S T U V W X Y Z A B C D
F  F G H I J K L M N O P Q R S T U V W X Y Z A B C D E
G  G H I J K L M N O P Q R S T U V W X Y Z A B C D E F
H  H I J K L M N O P Q R S T U V W X Y Z A B C D E F G
I  I J K L M N O P Q R S T U V W X Y Z A B C D E F G H
J  J K L M N O P Q R S T U V W X Y Z A B C D E F G H I
K  K L M N O P Q R S T U V W X Y Z A B C D E F G H I J
L  L M N O P Q R S T U V W X Y Z A B C D E F G H I J K
M  M N O P Q R S T U V W X Y Z A B C D E F G H I J K L
N  N O P Q R S T U V W X Y Z A B C D E F G H I J K L M
O  O P Q R S T U V W X Y Z A B C D E F G H I J K L M N
P  P Q R S T U V W X Y Z A B C D E F G H I J K L M N O
Q  Q R S T U V W X Y Z A B C D E F G H I J K L M N O P
R  R S T U V W X Y Z A B C D E F G H I J K L M N O P Q
S  S T U V W X Y Z A B C D E F G H I J K L M N O P Q R
T  T U V W X Y Z A B C D E F G H I J K L M N O P Q R S
U  U V W X Y Z A B C D E F G H I J K L M N O P Q R S T
V  V W X Y Z A B C D E F G H I J K L M N O P Q R S T U
W  W X Y Z A B C D E F G H I J K L M N O P Q R S T U V
X  X Y Z A B C D E F G H I J K L M N O P Q R S T U V W
Y  Y Z A B C D E F G H I J K L M N O P Q R S T U V W X
Z  Z A B C D E F G H I J K L M N O P Q R S T U V W X Y
```

cipher: **VVVRBACP**
key: **COVERCOVER...**
plaintext: **THANKYOU**

Polyalphabetic Ciphers

Although Vigenère claimed to have invented this cipher, the first cipher using lots of alphabets [known as a **polyalphabetic cipher**] is thought to have been developed earlier in fifteenth and sixteenth century Italy. There is even some evidence to suggest that Al-Kindi, the ninth century Arab mathematician who developed frequency analysis (see page 14), worked on the idea of creating polyalphabetic ciphers.

The Vigenère Cipher worked by using not one, but 26 Caesar Shifts, together with a secret key or password. Phew!

Crack the Vigenère Cipher

Can you decipher the Vigenère Cipher?

The message you need to send is a simple one: HELP. Spies and other people using ciphers call this the **'plaintext'**.

The key is:

The key is agreed with your spy partner beforehand.

Vigenère Square

A	B	C	D	E	F	G	H	I	J	K	L	M	N	O	P	Q	R	S	T	U	V	W	X	Y	Z
C	D	E	F	G	H	I	J	K	L	M	N	O	P	Q	R	S	T	U	V	W	X	Y	Z	A	B
O	P	Q	R	S	T	U	V	W	X	Y	Z	A	B	C	D	F	F	G	H	I	J	K	L	M	N
D	E	F	G	H	I	J	K	L	M	N	O	P	Q	R	S	T	U	V	W	X	Y	Z	A	B	C
E	F	G	H	I	J	K	L	M	N	O	P	Q	R	S	T	U	V	W	X	Y	Z	A	B	C	D

You can see the key has been highlighted in yellow and the message [plaintext] is highlighted in blue.

To work out the secret cipher word, or **encryption**, follow the first letter of the message [H] down to the line of the first letter of the key [C]. Where the H and C meet is the letter J. That is the first letter of your encryption.

Now, follow the other three letters of the message down from the top line until they reach the next line of the key. Can you work out the rest of the encryption?*

Think of your own message and use the Vigenère Cipher to work out the encryption.

I DON'T UNDERSTAND A WORD YOU'RE SAYING!

Not all codes are written down. In the nineteenth century, people living in the East End of London (Cockneys) developed a spoken secret language known as Cockney Rhyming Slang.

Cockney Rhyming Slang

Some people say Cockney Rhyming Slang was invented so that Cockneys could talk to each other without outsiders understanding what they were saying. Other people say it was a way for criminals to discuss their plans in secret without the police knowing what they were talking about. This is how it works. Say you want to code the word 'phone'. You take a phrase that rhymes with phone, like 'dog and bone' and the Cockney Rhyming Slang for a 'phone' becomes a 'dog and bone', or just 'dog'.

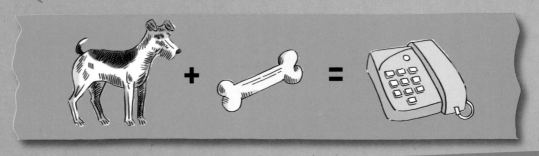

Secret Languages

Tennis players Heather Watson and Laura Robson used a secret language, backslang, to talk tactics when they were playing doubles. That way their opponents never knew what they were planning! Backslang is a code where words are reversed; so the backslang for 'tennis' is 'sinnet' and the backslang for 'boy' is - yes, you've guessed it - 'yob'!

Tennis players Heather Watson and Laura Robson on court. Do you think they're talking backslang?

Cockney Rhyming Slang

Some tricky Cockney Rhyming Slang phrases
leave off the last part of the phrase like this:

OBJECT	COCKNEY RHYMING SLANG PHRASE	EXAMPLE
Shirt	Uncle Bert	Ooh, I like your Uncle!
Stink	Pen and Ink	Cor! It really pens in here!
Gravy	Army and Navy	Pass the Army, will you?
Coat	Weasel and Stoat	It's freezing out! Put your weasel on.
Money	Bees and Honey	How much pocket bees do you get?

CODE BREAKER'S CORNER

Create Your Own Secret Language

Why not try using these secret languages
with your friends?

In the secret language 'Skimono Jive' you
add 'sk' to the beginning of every word. So:

> My teacher is an alien
> becomes
> Skmy skteacher skis skan skalien

Have a go! Skit's skeasy!

In the secret language 'Na' you add 'na' to the
end of every word. So:

> My teacher is an alien
> becomes
> Myna teacherna isna anna alienna

Mind you, in Na, 'banana' becomes er...
bananana, which is quite tricky to say!

THE MOST USEFUL CODE EVER INVENTED

In the early nineteenth century, people became interested in trying to send messages along electric wires. The trouble was that electrical current only works in two ways; either it's 'On' or it's 'Off'. So you could only send a message if it was no longer than two characters!

Morse Code

In the 1830s, an American painter named Samuel Morse hit on the idea of making codes for each letter of the alphabet using short and long bursts, or pulses, of electric current. Operators could then send messages down **telegraph wires** by tapping short pulses [dots] or long pulses [dashes] onto a machine. This became known as Morse Code.

A Morse Code operator taps the 'dots' and 'dashes' onto the keypad.

Right up until the middle of the last century, Morse Code was used on telegraph lines, undersea cables and radio circuits for most high-speed international communication.

The First Murderer Caught by Morse Code

Early in 1910, Dr Hawley Harvey Crippen was on the run from the police. He had murdered his wife and hidden her body in the cellar. Using disguises and false names, he escaped with his girlfriend and boarded a ship for Canada. However, the ship's captain thought he recognised him from newspaper pictures and, using Morse Code, sent an urgent message to Scotland Yard. Scotland Yard detectives got a faster ship and arrested Dr Crippen when he arrived in Canada.

International Morse Code

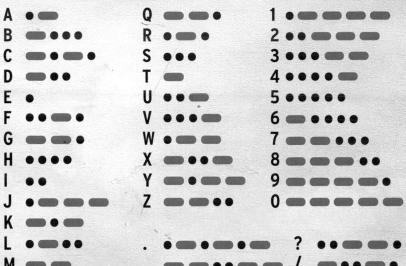

A	• —	Q	— — • —	1	• — — — —
B	— • • •	R	• — •	2	• • — — —
C	— • — •	S	• • •	3	• • • — —
D	— • •	T	—	4	• • • • —
E	•	U	• • —	5	• • • • •
F	• • — •	V	• • • —	6	— • • • •
G	— — •	W	• — —	7	— — • • •
H	• • • •	X	— • • —	8	— — — • •
I	• •	Y	— • — —	9	— — — — •
J	• — — —	Z	— — • •	0	— — — — —
K	— • —				
L	• — • •	.	• — • — • —	?	• • — — • •
M	— —	,	— — • • — —	/	— • • — •
N	— •	!	— • — • — —	=	— • • • —
O	— — —				
P	• — — •		SOS	• • • — — — • • •

Notice how Samuel Morse used frequency analysis to create his code.
The two most common letters each have just one symbol: E = • and T = —.
The least common letters have the longest codes and take longer to send.

Can You Read Morse Code?

You are a police officer at Scotland Yard in 1910. Can you decipher this Morse Code message and help catch the evil Dr Crippen?*

— • — •   • — • —   • •   • — — • —   • — — — •   •   — • —

• •   • • •   • —   • • — • • •   — — —   • —   • — •   — • • —

*Answer: Crippen is aboard

THE ANALYTICAL ENGINE

Remember Vigenère and his 'unbreakable' cipher (see pages 16-17)? Well, it turned out that it wasn't unbreakable after all. It was cracked in the nineteenth century by a British mathematician and cryptologist called Charles Babbage.

Charles Babbage was Professor of Mathematics at Cambridge University, a post once held by Sir Isaac Newton and now held by Professor Sir Stephen Hawking!

Charles Babbage

Charles Babbage was fascinated by numbers and coding and wondered if it would be possible for a properly coded machine to do mathematical calculations. He ended up designing what he called the Analytical Engine. It used coding and had a central processing unit [CPU] and separate memory, just like a modern computer.

Ada Lovelace

Very few people could understand how the Analytical Engine worked, but one person who did was Ada Lovelace. From an early age, Ada had been interested in maths. She came from a rich family, and although it was highly unusual at that time for girls to be allowed to study anything, Ada's mother paid for her to have maths lessons. When she was 18, she met Charles Babbage. She became interested in the Analytical Engine and wrote an **algorithm** [step-by-step instructions] for using it. These were the first ever instructions that could be used to control a computing device.

Ada Lovelace was the world's first computer programmer. The top secret coding language now used by the United States Military is called 'Ada', in her memory.

Maths Codes

Ada Lovelace loved maths puzzles. One famous maths puzzle that she probably came across was invented by the German mathematician Carl Gauss, while he was still at primary school! This is the puzzle: how quickly can you add up all the numbers between I and I00? It's so easy!

Add up the first and last numbers and you get I0I:
I + I00 = I0I

$$1 + 100 = 101$$

Add up the next to first and next to last numbers and you still get this:
2 + 99 = I0I

$$2 + 99 = 101$$

And so on:
3 + 98 = I0I
4 + 97 = I0I

$$3 + 98 = 101$$

In fact, you end up with 50 lots of I0I, giving a total of 5050.

Now you can impress your friends and teachers with your quick maths skills!

$$4 + 97 = 101$$

Charles Babbage never managed to get the money to make a full-sized Analytical Engine, but he did build a model of it which can be seen at the Science Museum in London.

THE ENIGMA MACHINE

In the 1920s, German cryptologists invented a cipher machine to keep their army, navy and air force messages secret. They called the machine Enigma, from the Greek word for 'mystery'.

Cracking the Code

Enigma could put a message into code in over 150,000,000,000 ways; a bit different to the Caesar Shift code, which had just 25 options! Enigma codes were changed every day. The Germans believed that they were unbreakable. What they didn't know was that a team of Polish code breakers was already working on ways to crack the codes. When the Second World War broke out in 1939, they passed the information to British and French code breakers.

This is an Enigma machine. An electric current went from the keyboard through a set of rotors to light up the 'code' alphabet.

Bletchley Park

The British code breaking headquarters was at Bletchley Park, about 50 miles north of London. The code breakers there soon realised that a code that had been created by a machine could only be deciphered with the help of a machine.

Bletchley Park was the top secret home of British code breaking during the Second World War.

24

Bombes

The machines that were built to try and break Enigma were called bombes; not because they tended to blow up, but because, being mechanical, they were as a noisy as bombs. The codes would first be converted into numbers and then be analysed by a bombe. The new decoded numbers would then be converted back into text and – finally – translated into English.

As the war went on, thousands of men and women were drafted into Bletchley Park to work on deciphering the Enigma codes with bombe machines.

CODE BREAKER'S CORNER

Tricky Translations

Even after the day's Enigma codes had been deciphered there was still work to be done. Teams of translators had to translate the messages from the language in which they'd been sent into English.

What language do you think these Enigma messages have been sent in? And what do think they say? (It's the same message in each language.)*

1 Angriff in der Dämmerung

2 明け方に攻撃 / Akegata ni kogeki

3 Attacco all'alba

*Answer: 1.German 2. Japanese 3. Italian
The message says 'Attack at dawn'.

25

THE COMPUTER AS BIG AS A ROOM

As the Second World War dragged on, Bletchley Park was receiving, on average, 3,000 messages a day to decipher. The bombes couldn't cope.

Alan Turing

Alan Turing, a mathematician who worked at Bletchley Park and who had been involved in building the bombes, decided to try and design an even bigger decoding machine. He came up with a machine which was the size of a room. It was called Colossus, after the giant Greek statue. It was built by a team of telephone engineers and could work at 5000 characters a second. It was the world's first electronic computer. Towards the end of the war, Colossus 2 was built. It was five times faster than Colossus 1.

Alan Turing first became interested in codes and computing when, as a student, he read Ada Lovelace's notes, written a hundred years before, about the Analytical Machine.

Early computers like Colossus and Charles Babbage's Analytical Engine worked by deciphering text by 'reading' small holes punched in a card. Different sequences of holes stood for different letters; similar to the way the dots and dashes of Morse Code work.

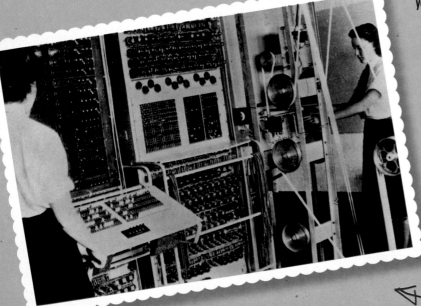

Computer operators feed data into Colossus.

A complete Mark 2 Colossus machine can be seen at the Bletchley Park Code Breaking Centre Museum.

Ultra Messages

Some of the messages deciphered at Bletchley Park were so secret they were classified as Ultra. Ultra messages could only be read by a few top people in the wartime government. The man who delivered the Ultra messages to London was a naval officer, Lieutenant Commander Ian Fleming. After the war Ian Fleming became an author: he wrote the James Bond spy novels!

CODE BREAKER'S CORNER

Word Games

The code breakers and cryptologists at Bletchley Park enjoyed playing word games. Can you decipher these **anagrams** [the letters are in the wrong order]? Put the letters in the correct order to discover the word. They all relate to Bletchley Park.*

SOLOSUCS	IAMGEN
MEBBO	TLUAR

*Answers: Colossus, Enigma, Bombe, Ultra

Tu INfINiTY hND BEYOND

Today, codes are everywhere. Very few of the codes we use today are about secrets, though. They are all about machines communicating with each other, and with us.

Binary Code

Everything that operates digitally uses codes: not just computers, but also phones, televisions, and even dishwashers. Every piece of digital hardware is descended from Charles Babbage's Analytical Engine and Alan Turing's Colossus. All the coded information in the computer's processing system, whether it's text, music or graphics, is stored using Binary Code.

Like Charles Babbage's punched cards and Morse Code, Binary Code uses just two symbols. Here, 0 and 1 are being used by a computer programmer.

DeepMind playing the board game 'Go'.

DeepMind

But what of the future? Two hundred years ago, people laughed at Ada Lovelace when she predicted that in the future advanced coding techniques would enable computers to compose music. Today, computers like DeepMind are being taught to play board games – and to get very good at them. Scientists are predicting that by 2050 computers will have reached human level intelligence. All of this is achieved through coding.

The Leetspeak Cipher

Leet, or I337, is a cipher used for emailing and texting. In Leet, letters and sounds are replaced by numbers and common symbols that you find on a keyboard or phone. Often the cipher looks like the letter it is representing; so B is represented by 8. In Leet the letter L is represented by I, E by 3 and T by 7; so Leet is written as I337. Numbers and symbols used in Leet are changing all the time, but here is a typical version of Leetspeak:

A = 4, /=\, @, ^, //-\\   B = 8,]3,]8, |3, |8,]]3   C = (, {, [[, <, €

D =), [}, |), |>, [>,]])   E = 3, ii, €   F = I=, (=,]]=, ph

G = 6, 9, (_>, [[6, &, (,   H = #, |-|, (-),)-(, }{, }-{   I = 1, !, |,][, []

J = _I, u|, ;_[], ;_[[K = I<, |{,][<,]]<, []<   L = | , 1, |_, []_,][_, £

M = ΛΛ , /V\, |V|, [V], (V)   N = /V, |\|, (\), /|/, [\]   O = 0, (), [], <>, *, [[]]

P = |D, |*, |>, []D,][D   Q = (,) or 0, or 0   R = |2, |?, |-,]]2, []2,

S = 5, $, š   T = 7, +, ']', 7', ~|~, -|-   U = (_), |_|, _\, /_/

V = V, \W/, √   W = VV, |^|, [^], (^), ///   X = ><

Y = '/,, %, '/, \j, "//   Z = 2, z, 7_, '/_

Try decoding this Leetspeak cipher*:

7 # 3 ΛΛ ! 1 I< 5 # 4 I< 3 5   4 I2 3   ! /V   7 #3   I= I2 !) 6 3

GLOSSARY

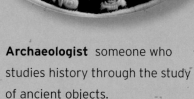

Algorithm a set of instructions that you need to follow to solve a problem. Programmers write algorithms to enable computers to complete tasks.

Anagram a word or phrase made up of rearranging the letters of another word. For example: rearrange the letters in 'listen' and you get 'silent'.

Archaeologist someone who studies history through the study of ancient objects.

Code a way of communicating something using numbers, letters or symbols that stand for something else. Some, but not all, codes are secret.

Cipher a way of sending secret messages using single letters, numbers or symbols.

Cryptologist someone who studies codes; how to make them and how to decipher them.

Decipher to work out the meaning of a code.

Encryption the process of putting plaintext [your message] into a code.

Frequency analysis deciphering a code by working out which are the most common letters, numbers or symbols used.

Glyph a picture or symbol that represents a word or a sound. Glyph is usually used to mean a symbol that is carved. In computing a glyph is a small graphic symbol.

Hieroglyph a picture or symbol that represents a word or a sound.

Microdot a microphotograph, often of a document, about the size of a pinhead.

Pig pen cipher a cipher that uses squares. So called because it is meant to look like a drawing of the enclosures where farmers would keep their pigs.

Pixel a tiny part of a display screen, one of many which make up a larger image.

FURTHER INFORMATION

Plaintext text that isn't in code.

Polyalphabetic cipher a cipher that uses more than one alphabet.

Steganography the practice of hiding secret messages in pictures, text or computer data.

Substitution cipher a cipher where one letter is changed for another.

Telegraph wires wires along which messages can be transmitted using electricity.

Tracking following someone without being seen.

Transposition cipher a cipher where the word or letter order is changed.

Books to Read

How to be an International Spy
by Lonely Planet Kids (2015)

The Spy Book
by Dorling Kindersley (2011)

Places to Visit

You can see the Rosetta Stone at **The British Museum**.
www.britishmuseum.org

You can see a model of Charles Babbage's Analytical Engine at the **Science Museum**.
www.sciencemuseum.org.uk

You can visit **Bletchley Park**; the home of British code breaking and the birthplace of modern information technology.
www.bletchleypark.org.uk

INDEX

algorithm 22

Al-Kindi 14, 16

alphabet 7, 10, 11, 12, 14, 15, 16, 17, 20, 21, 24

anagrams 27

Analytical Engine 22-23, 26, 28

Ancient Egyptians 6

Ancient Greeks 8, 9, 10, 12

Ancient Romans 10, 11

Babbage, Charles 22-23, 26, 28

Babington Plot 14

backslang 18

barcode 7

Binary code 28

Bletchley Park 24, 25, 27

bombes 25, 26

Caesar Shift 10-11, 24

cave paintings 4, 5

Cockney Rhyming Slang 18-19

Colossus 26-27, 28

cryptologists 16, 22, 24, 27

DeepMind 28

electrical current 20

encryption 17

Enigma code 24-25, 26-27

First World War 12

frequency analysis 14-15, 16, 21

glyphs 6

hieroglyphs 6

invisible ink 9

Leetspeak 29

Lovelace, Ada 22-23, 26, 28

Maya 6

microdots 9

Morse code 20-21, 26, 28

Napoleon 13

pictures 4, 5, 6-7, 9

pig pen cipher 13

pixels 9

plaintext 16, 17

polyalphabetical cipher 16-17

Polybius' Square 12

postcode 7

Rosetta Stone, the 6

Scouting 5

Second World War 24-25, 26-27

Skimono Jive 19

smoke signals 12

steganography 8

substitution cipher 10-11, 16

torches 12

tracking 5

transposition cipher 15

Turing, Alan 26, 28

Vigenère Cipher 16-17, 22

writing backwards 10-11